Bold Choice

They Say I'm Bad

Terri M. Bolds, MS, LPC

Illustrated by Mike D. Gray

Copyright © 2017 by Terri M. Bolds
All rights reserved.
Printed and Bound in the United States

Published by
Bold Visions Consulting
(513) 299-8177
www.boldvisionsconsulting.com

Cover and Interior Illustrations: Mike D. Gray
Cover & Interior Layout: TWA Solutions.com

Second Printing: May 2019
ISBN: 978-1-7330563-1-1

All rights reserved. No part of this book may be reproduced, stored in a retrieval system or transmitted in any form or by any means without the prior written permission of the publisher—except by a reviewer who may quote brief passages in a review to be printed in a newspaper, magazine or journal.

For inquiries, speaking engagements, book signings, literary events, contact: boldcounselor3@gmail.com.

To all of my nephews and nieces: Antwan, MonDayll, MonTrae, Micah, Mielle, Aiden, Casmier, Aniyah, and Ariah, always remember you have a choice.

Love you, TT, "Aunt Terri"

"As your teacher, I am concerned about all my students, and that means you are important to me. I want to understand why you display the same disruptive behavior every day."

"Because they say I'm bad."

"Micah, let's talk and work together to find a solution to help you."

Mrs. Heart learned that Micah was the older of two children in the family and that he felt he was letting his parents down. Micah shared an example of his mom's punishing him for not completing all of his chores. He also felt his sister received more help with her homework than he did.

Sometimes, Micah would purposely not walk the dog or fold his clothes because he felt that no matter what he did, he would be perceived as "bad."

He explained that if he wasn't tough, his dad wouldn't talk to him. Although his dad was a football fan, Micah didn't like football and never scored.

Micah also shared that he didn't have friends. He had been so mean to the other kids, he didn't think anyone would want to be his friend.

Micah and Mrs. Heart began to develop a plan to help him address his challenges. In the middle of the conversation, Micah stood up and said, "I don't know why you are talking to me. You just think I'm bad too."

"Micah, everyone does not have negative feelings about you. Instead of saying 'good' or 'bad,' let's say 'healthy behavior' or 'unhealthy behavior.'

"Let's make a list of healthy and unhealthy behaviors. Let's start with the unhealthy list. What are some of your unhealthy behaviors?"

Micah began to list them: yelling, throwing things, not listening to adults. Then he began the healthy behavior list: helping, sharing, completing tasks.

Afterwards, Micah and Mrs. Heart discussed the lists. Micah was able to explain what he had written under healthy and unhealthy behaviors. Mrs. Heart and Micah role played different scenarios as an interactive way of learning. For example, Micah helping Mrs. Heart pass out papers or helping classmates when they need help in class. Mrs. Heart praised Micah for the work he completed regarding understanding his behaviors. She reminded Micah that he is capable of changing his behavior and that she believes in his ability to do so.

Meanwhile, the rest of Micah's class was returning from recess. Zion appeared in the class earlier than expected and requested to speak with Mrs. Heart. Zion, who had been diagnosed with ADHD, worked privately with Mrs. Heart about ways to pay attention and not be disruptive during class time. Micah thought that Zion was weird, he had repeatedly teased him.

When Zion smiled at Micah and complimented him on the work he was doing on the chalkboard, Micah was confused. "How come you're talking to me? I am mean to you all the time. I just laughed at you today when you fell and dropped all of your books and glasses."

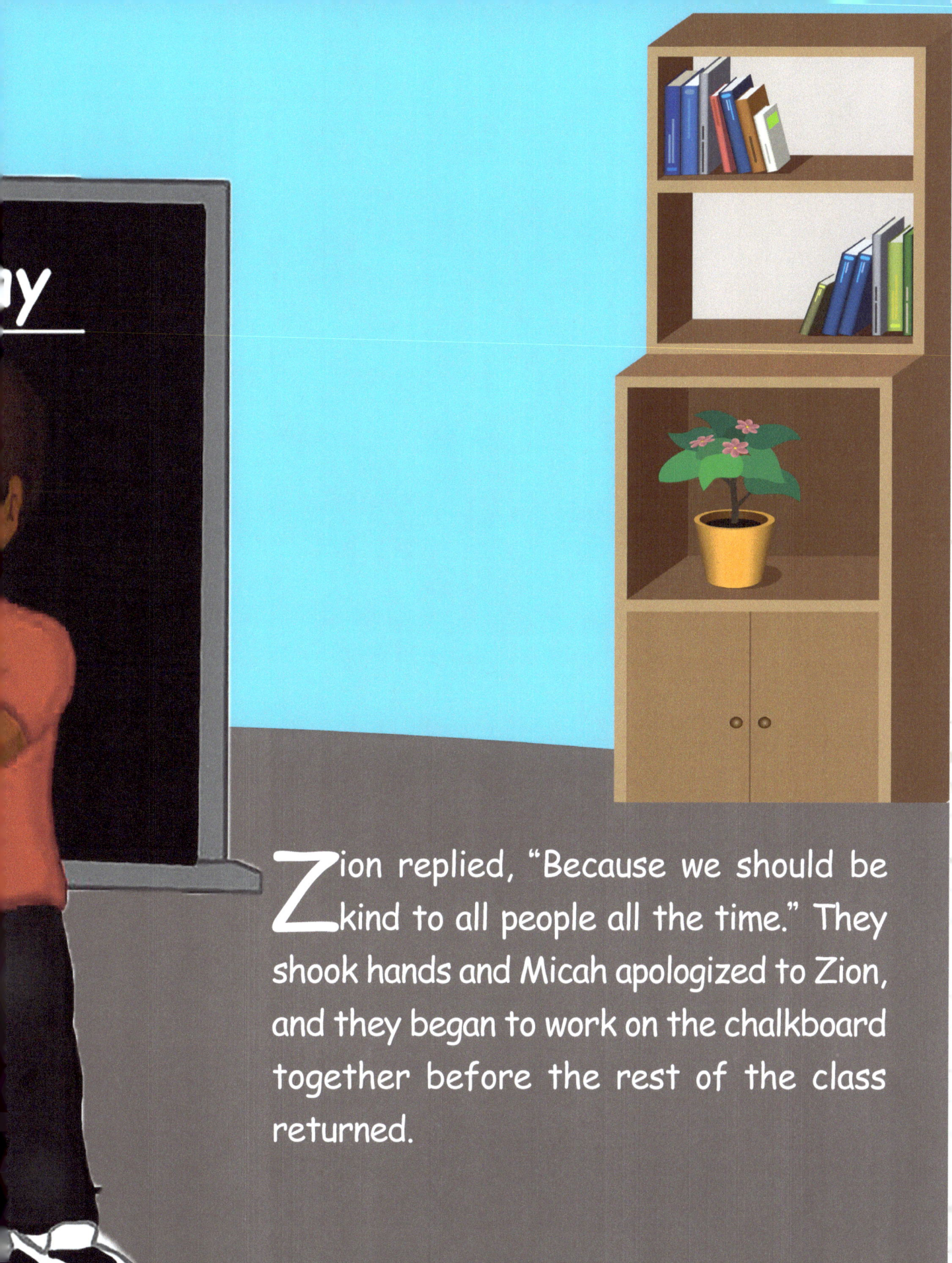

Zion replied, "Because we should be kind to all people all the time." They shook hands and Micah apologized to Zion, and they began to work on the chalkboard together before the rest of the class returned.

Mrs. Heart had previously scheduled a meeting with Micah and his parents after school. Micah's father, Mr. Love, owned two car repair shops, and his mother, Mrs. Love, was a registered nurse. They both worked a lot.

When they attended the conference, they learned that their son felt he was "bad" because that's what they called him whenever he messed up. Mrs. Heart

encouraged Micah to share his feelings with his parents in a healthy manner. Micah was able to express feelings of sadness calmly and without yelling.

Micah began to express the feeling that his father was not proud of him because he never wanted to do anything with him and yelled at him all the time. He felt that his mother wished he were a better child.

That day, each person in Micah's family learned something. Micah's parents learned the power of words. They saw that by calling Micah "bad," they had given him the idea that all he could ever be was bad. Micah also learned that if he has a problem, he can always talk to his parents.

Micah's father apologized for being so hard on him and explained that he was being strict with him because his father had been strict. Micah's father learned that each person must be treated as an individual. The way his father had raised him was not appropriate for Micah.

Micah's mother did not know that the expectations she had set for her son were overwhelming. She decided to have a family meeting about ways the whole family could share home responsibilities.

Micah's father gave him a big embrace and assured him that he loved everything about him and was especially proud of his bravery and willingness to express his feelings.

Micah shared what he learned about healthy and unhealthy behaviors and told his parents he would begin to make better decisions.

Micah also learned a lesson in forgiveness and kindness. He thought that because he was mean to other kids, they would never want to play with him, but Zion showed Micah that his theory was false. When we make mistakes, we do not become worthless. There will be many opportunities to make healthy decisions.

    Micah learned that communication can resolve problems.

    Everyone makes mistakes and has the chance to learn from those mistakes and try again and again and again.

www.ingramcontent.com/pod-product-compliance
Lightning Source LLC
Chambersburg PA
CBHW041122070526
44584CB00002B/246